Crystal Healing

A Complete Guide to Healing with Crystals

Jamie Parr

Table of Contents

Introduction

Crystal healing is a widely respected form of healing that has been used for many generations. Although it is commonly referred to as a form of "alternative healing", crystal healing was viewed as being a common form of healing back in the day. Cultures and religions from all around the world relied on crystals as a way to create space for divine healing to happen within those who were suffering mentally, emotionally, physically, or spiritually. There were no known boundaries as to how crystals could help with one's ailments, as they were believed to offer a myriad of benefits to people in need.

These days, crystal healing may not be as common as it once was, but it is still just as powerful. Teaching yourself the ways of crystal healing is a wonderful way to supplement modern medicine and healing practices, so you can experience deeper healing that targets you all the way to your core energies. In discovering how to embrace crystal healing, you will also discover how you can play a more active role in caring for yourself in a deeper and more meaningful way.

As you read through this book, I encourage you to understand that crystal healing is something that requires a great deal of respect, understanding, and consideration in order for it to work. You must be open and receptive to the energies of the crystals if you wish to experience the full scope of the benefits they offer.

The deeper you can allow crystals to penetrate your energy field through acceptance and allowance, the deeper your healing will be. When the core of a problem has been adequately healed, then you know the problem will not return. In this sense, unlike a large portion of modern medicine, crystals are not used to simply treat symptoms. Rather, crystals focus on the core of health ailments, working to heal you in an all-encompassing fashion.

If you are ready to discover how you can embrace the ancient art of crystal healing and use it in your own daily life, it's time to begin!

Chapter 1: What Is Crystal Healing?

Crystal healing was, at one time, one of the primary healing methods, alongside herbal healing and other practical and spiritual healing measures. Crystal healing is not popular among medicinal doctors and scientists, as they often refer to crystal healing as being a form of pseudoscience. The reality, however, is that many people have personally experienced the benefits of crystals and feel far better after they experience crystal healing. There are many reports of miraculous recoveries from a myriad of symptoms following a crystal healing treatment. Although there may not be any studies directly showing the correlation, it is hard to deny the number of people who report feeling far better after using crystal healing methods.

How Crystal Healing Works

Crystal healing is said to work through a method called absorption and energy resonance. The short explanation is that anytime you set a crystal near you, it vibrates at a specific frequency and encourages your body to vibrate at that same frequency. Individuals wear crystals as varying forms of jewelry, hold them in their pockets, and decorate their homes with them as a way to absorb the resonance of the specific crystal they are working with.

The longer explanation is a little more complex. The idea is that each individual crystal has its own unique vibrational frequency, caused by the same life force energy that moves through you. In a sense, they are describing the "spirit" of the crystal itself, suggesting that the spirit holds a vibrational frequency, much like your spirit does. This particular belief is rooted in the fact that your nervous system, or a system built on electrical impulses, is associated with your crown chakra, which is closely linked to your source energy. Many crystal healers believe that the energy that moves through your body, as well as everything else on earth, is the embodiment of the connection we share with source energy or the source energy that we hold within ourselves.

The belief, then, is that when you work with a crystal, the energy resonance of that crystal, or it's spirit, interacts with the energy resonance of your body, or your spirit. As crystals are absolute, meaning they experience no emotions or other subjective experiences, they maintain a similar energy at all times. They are far more difficult to push off of their typical energy resonance than you are, so by keeping one around you, the energy resonance of that crystal pulls your energy into its correct resonance, too. Of course, a crystal's energy resonance can be sidetracked, which means you must cleanse your crystals from time to time to heal any disruptions they may be experiencing in their energy field.

During a treatment session, crystals are often placed directly near problem points in the body, or on body parts where you want that energy to resonate. For example, during a reiki session that has been combined with a crystal healing session, the practitioner may place crystals along your chakra pillar with the crystals directly corresponding to the chakras they are placed next to. The closer the crystal is to the problem area, the better it is believed to work. Naturally, you need to keep the crystal nearby the problem area for long enough for it to work on that part of your body and bring healing energy to your system.

The Possible Scientific Explanation

While most scientists do not agree with the aforementioned explanation, that does not mean it is false. While scientists do not explain the effects of crystals in the same way that practitioners do, doesn't mean that scientists deny the benefits of crystals altogether. Scientists who have researched crystal healing often agree that the likely reason why crystal healing works is due to what is commonly called a "placebo effect." Before you write this off as meaning that crystal healing is not genuine, read on.

The placebo effect suggests that people who believe they are being treated end up experiencing benefits from the proposed treatment, even if the treatment is not a true treatment method, because of a certain experience they have in their brains. Essentially, their belief in the treatment is so strong that it results in their brain triggering healing to occur, alleviating them from their problematic symptoms.

Regardless of how scientists explain it, many agree that crystals have the capacity to create seemingly miraculous healing benefits in some of those who try them. This means that crystal healing may be explained by the placebo effect as far as science is concerned, but it still has the capacity to have very real impacts on your physical body. There is also the possibility that scientists are simply yet to find a way to measure the method through which crystals are able to heal.

If you are willing to accept that crystals work in a seemingly magical and often unexplainable manner, you are likely to be one of the many who experiences powerful healing benefits from these crystals. Regardless of *how* they work, it is undeniable that millions of people throughout history, all the way up to modern times have experienced benefits from this healing method.

The Safety Factor

You may wonder if crystal healing is safe, especially considering there are certification courses practitioners can take in order to work with crystals on the physical body. Fortunately, crystal healing is absolutely safe, and the likelihood of it becoming dangerous is slim.

It is important to note that crystal healers, specifically, are not required to have any specific training, neither relating to crystals, health, or anything else associated with crystal healing. While many do choose to take a certification course, they are not required to. The only time courses may be required, or specific licensing may be required, is if someone intends on incorporating crystal healing into other practices like massage or anything else. Similarly, if you intend on offering crystal healing sessions to others, which will result in you touching their bodies at all with these crystals, your hands, or any other tools, you may need specific licenses, training, and insurance to protect the legality of your practice.

Aside from the legality, there are two specific risk factors that you need to be aware of in order to protect your health and the health of anyone planning to use crystals. The first risk factor is the specific crystal being used. Certain crystals are made of minerals or materials that are dangerous for the human body, meaning they should not touch the skin or be on the skin for prolonged periods. You should also refrain from drinking water or other drinks that have been "infused" with the crystals, as harmful properties may have leached into the water and could result in the water being toxic to your health.

The second consideration is the fact that many will consider foregoing medical support in favor of receiving help through crystal healing, instead. No condition, especially one that could be life-threatening, should ever be ignored or treated with alternative practices before first speaking with your doctor as medicine will always work faster than crystal healing. Even ethically trained crystal healing practitioners will agree that medical support should be sought first to treat the symptoms, and that crystal healing can be used to improve treatment while also helping treat the root cause.

In other words, crystal healing should always be used to supplement medical practices or, used in areas where medical support is not necessary or relevant. For example, diabetes should be worked on first with the help of your doctor, then supplemented through the use of crystals. However, something more minor such as stress headaches or minor sinus congestion can be treated exclusively through crystal healing.

Chapter 2: A Basic Crystal Healing Set

As you get started with crystal healing, it can be helpful to start by building out a basic crystal healing set. This set will be comprised of crystals that are useful for an array of symptoms you might experience in your body, and that can be used to create healing within your energy field. These crystals are best used on a regular basis but can also be used over longer intentional healing sessions.

Building Your First Set

The bare minimum you need for a crystal set is obviously the crystals themselves, and a pouch to carry them in. However, you might also want to include other things in your set, like Palo Santo or sage, other healing herbs, chakra healing cards, or an amulet or talisman you have made for yourself. Another great thing to include in your crystal healing set is a small print out of what all of the crystals mean and how they can be used to maximize the healing benefits you gain from them. This way, you know how to use them on the go, and you won't have to research your crystals every time you want to use your set.

The following crystals should be included in your healing set: black tourmaline, citrine, carnelian, aventurine, lapis lazuli, tiger eye, clear quartz, amethyst, and rose quartz. These are all excellent for a beginner's set, as they have easy-to-remember uses and are strong yet subtle in their energy, meaning they can be helpful without being overwhelming. I suggest you master working with all of these crystals before moving onto working with any other, more powerful crystals.

Black Tourmaline

Black tourmaline is a jet-black stone that corresponds with your root chakra. If you need protection combined with the ability to deeply ground your energies, this is the crystal to reach for. In addition to helping ground your root chakra, black tourmaline will also help draw your sacral and solar plexus chakras into alignment, as it is well-known for working with the three lower chakras. As you work with this crystal, you will find your sense of self-confidence and ability to embrace who you are deepening, as you realize it is safe for you to exist as you are. This crystal can be held in your hand, from which it can absorb any negative energies within your body or space. You can also wear it as a piece of jewelry for ongoing protection from unwanted energies throughout your day.

Citrine

Citrine comes in a variety of yellow tones, ranging from pale to golden yellow. Some are like honey in color, or nearly brown, while others contain rainbow or sparkly sections in them. Citrine is known for connecting with the sacral chakra, and it has the ability to aid with happiness, prosperity, generosity, creativity, pleasure, and confidence. This crystal is well-known for helping you let go of negative behavior patterns, ease depression, and eliminate fears and phobias you might experience. Citrine can also help you balance your emotions, so you experience more peace in your life. You can meditate with citrine by holding it over your sacral chakra as you meditate, or by wearing it on a necklace to keep it in your immediate energy field throughout the day.

Carnelian

Carnelian is also associated with your sacral chakra. This deep red stone occasionally has white dredged through it, and it is used for emotional stability, sociability, creativity, individuality, and memory. Carnelian can also encourage feelings of harmony, courage, happiness, and self-esteem. Some healers use carnelian in rebirth, reincarnation, and past life recall sessions because of how closely related to the sacral chakra it is. The best way to use carnelian is to wear it as a piece of jewelry, as this allows the gentle energy to stay with you for the duration of your healing session. You can also wear carnelian as earrings or as a necklace to promote sexuality and fertility during moments of intimacy with a lover.

Aventurine

Aventurine is a beautiful green stone that is closely linked to your heart chakra. Alternative pieces of aventurine come in the colors blue and yellow, though green is by far the most common. Aventurine can be used to help promote your independence and calmness, as well as to support your circulation and ease symptoms of congestion. If you have stammers or stress-related ticks, aventurine can help you experience relief from these symptoms. Aventurine is another crystal that should be worn throughout the day so that you may receive ongoing benefits from this crystal. Wearing it as a necklace keeps it close to your heart chakra, but bracelets made of aventurine are particularly helpful, too. You can also meditate with aventurine or, keep it next to your bed as a way to assist you with all things relating to your emotions, as well as heart health.

Lapis Lazuli

Lapis lazuli is associated with your throat chakra, due to its deep blue coloring. However, some also associate this crystal with your third eye chakra because of how royal and mystical it looks. Lapis can encourage you to express yourself in a more honest and authentic manner, while also boosting your feelings of compassion and morality. When you need to speak your truth, or you are facing a situation where you need to communicate in a large, powerful manner, bringing lapis lazuli with you is a great way to receive the assistance you need. Meditate with lapis lazuli over your throat chakra as a way to maximize the benefits you gain from it or, wear it as a necklace during any time where you might find yourself experiencing a greater need to communicate with clarity, honesty, and compassion.

Tiger Eye

Tiger eye is a powerful protection stone that is associated with your root chakra, though it is often used to protect your energy field as a whole. This crystal is also said to bring good luck to anyone who wears it, so keeping a piece on you throughout the day can be highly beneficial. The easiest way to use tiger eye is to keep a piece in your pocket or to wear it as a bracelet, as this keeps it low and close to your root chakra. Beyond protection and bringing good luck your way, tiger eye can help promote mental clarity, assist you with boosting your logical reasoning, and support you with healing psychosomatic illnesses, fear, and anxiety. Because of how powerful tiger eye can be, it is advised that you only use it as needed when you first begin to work with crystals, otherwise its energy might be overwhelming.

Clear Quartz

Clear quartz is a "mother of all" type crystal, working well with every chakra on your entire chakra pillar, and beyond. This crystal can be used in two ways when it is inside your basic healing kit. Inside of the pouch, clear quartz will help cleanse and balance other crystals, as it is said to be a powerful energy healer and cleanser, particularly for other energy tools you might work with. Clear quartz can also be used to promote your psychic abilities, purify the energy in other chakras, or calm your energies if you find you are feeling overwhelmed or out of sorts. Anytime you are experiencing brain fog or difficulty remembering and visualizing things, incorporate clear quartz into your healing routine as a way to clarify your energy and your vision.

Amethyst

Amethyst is another highly protective stone, though the way it protects is far different from stones like tiger eye or black tourmaline. Instead of absorbing or deflecting negative energy, amethyst works directly with your third eye to help "dodge" unwanted energy that could lead to you experiencing a psychic attack, or that could lead to addictions. This stone is said to be highly effective at purifying your energy field so you can experience relief from unwanted visions or emotional or mental overwhelm, all of which can lead to addictive behaviors in individuals. You can wear amethyst during the day, especially while working with your third eye, to help protect your energy field. It can also be used to help dissipate cravings or addictions you might be experiencing. For this, simply hold it in your hand

and meditate with it until you begin to experience freedom from said craving.

Rose Quartz

Rose quartz is said to be the "hug of the universe." This light pink quartz is directly associated with the heart chakra and your emotions, and has the capacity to help you confidently navigate your emotions in a positive, lasting way. You can use rose quartz to help bring trust and harmony back into relationships, including your relationship with yourself. It can also be used to support you through challenges you may face, such as depression, grief, loss, anger, anxiety, overwhelm, and any other emotions you might experience. If you yearn for greater feelings of peace in any area of your life, rose quartz is the stone to reach for.

Chapter 3: Precious Healing Crystals

After you have mastered working with the basic healing crystals, it can be nice to acquire advanced healing crystals or more precious healing crystals. These crystals are often more expensive, rare, and difficult to acquire because they are meant to be used for more advanced healing practices. You should not acquire or use any of these crystals before you know how to work with basic crystals and crystal energy, because these crystals can carry with them intense energy. While crystals are generally safe to work with, they can bring with them overwhelming energy, which can lead to vivid dreams, visions, as well as other intense feelings that may feel unusual or difficult to navigate. Further, you should know how to properly store these crystals before working with them, as that ensures that you are safely preserving their energy, and yours.

What Are Advanced Crystals?

Advanced crystals are crystals that tend to contain more intense forms of energy, and that can work in deeper and more profound ways. You can use these crystals in the same way you would use any other crystal, whether it be meditating with them, wearing them, or keeping them in your vicinity. With advanced crystals however, it is important you keep them separate from each other, and that you keep them away from your physical space unless you are intentionally working with them, as their combined energies can become overwhelming. Reports of people experiencing nightmares, anxiety, and overactive imaginations have all stemmed from people keeping too many advanced crystals with conflicting energies near each other, and near their physical person. The following advanced crystals are excellent to start with. When adding them to your collection, choose ones that contain energies you need or want to work with. This way, you can keep your collection intentional and personalized.

Ametrine

Ametrine is a crystal associated with both the solar plexus and crown chakras. This crystal is a mixture of amethyst and citrine and brings about the natural healing powers of both crystals. Use it to relieve stress, expand your spiritual awareness, improve your creativity, and heal your inner strength. Meditate with it on your chest or wear it as a necklace to keep it between your solar plexus and crown chakras, so they both benefit from your using this particular crystal. If you have been particularly stressed, sleeping with a piece near your bed or under your pillow is a wonderful way to navigate your symptoms.

Angel Aura Quartz

Angel aura quartz is a beautiful clear, and rainbow-colored stone with what crystal collectors call "flash." Flash means that when light hits the crystal, it changes colors or becomes more vibrant in that particular area. Angel aura quartz is a wonderful tool for integration and insight. You can use this crystal to enhance your psychic powers or to draw more light energy into your physical body. To do this, set a piece of angel aura quartz in front of you at around eye level, and meditate while you gaze at it. The power of the crystal will infuse with the power of your body, enhancing your powers and increasing your light absorption.

Angelite

Angelite is a stunning light blue and white stone that looks somewhat like a cloudy sky. This crystal should never be exposed to water as it will turn into Gypsum, which will damage its healing properties. Angelite is known for strengthening your organs, improving your creativity, and increasing your inner guidance. You can also use it to improve your astral travel experiences, which you can learn more about in my book *Astral Projection*. To benefit from angelite, it is best to wear it as a piece of jewelry. This crystal is also often turned in crystal spheres, which can be kept nearby or held in your hands to improve your meditation practise and balance your energy.

Auralite

Auralite is a form of amethyst that is said to be one of the most powerful crystals in existence. This crystal was discovered in Canada in 2007, and is now one of the most popular crystals in the world, often being called the "Master Healer." This variation of amethyst can assist you with manifesting in the most powerful way possible, which is why you should be highly careful when working with it. "Be careful what you wish for, because you might actually get it" is a great phrase to consider when you plan on bringing this crystal into your space. Be highly intentional to attract healing and positive outcomes for all involved, as you never want to manifest bad things into your life, or into the lives of others.

Eudialyte

Eudialyte is a highly specific crystal that works directly on your ability to experience clairaudient experiences. It can also be used to improve your ability to experience coincidences and synchronicities in your life. It is advised that you refrain from using eudialyte unless you have intentionally activated and worked with your third eye chakra. Otherwise, you might find yourself overwhelmed by the energy of this crystal. The best way to work with eudialyte is to meditate with it or to wear it during periods where you want to have psychic experiences, as this ensures that you are only activating these energies and powers when you want to, and not sporadically.

Herkimer Diamond

Herkimer diamonds are becoming more popular as people opt for Herkimer diamonds over other diamonds, which are known for being unethically sourced and as a result contain bad energy. Using Herkimer diamonds for crystal healing specifically is best when you need healing associated with your spiritual energy. This crystal is often used as an "attunement stone" to help attune your energies to one another, or to the energies of others around you. Wear it on a ring, as earrings, or keep a piece on you as a way to receive the benefits of this crystal on an ongoing basis.

Jadeite

Jadeite is a type of jade, as you might have guessed. This crystal is especially powerful when it comes to recalling, analyzing, and connecting to your dreams. If you come across a deity carved into jadeite, it is believed to be a powerful crystal for protection and good fortune. Anytime you are doing dreamwork, keep a piece of jadeite handy for that work. It will help you navigate your dreams in a peaceful, calm, yet powerful manner.

Lemurian

Lemurian crystal is a clear crystal that looks similar to quartz but has a different makeup. This crystal is another "Master Healer" as it is said to be useful in manifesting healing in any area of your life. Another particularly profound use for Lemurian is that it is said to help telepathically transmit messages to and from Lemuria, which is a long-lost continent that sunk underwater many years ago. You can also use this crystal to improve your telepathic communications in other areas of your life, making it a powerful crystal to use during psychic sessions.

Marcasite

Marcasite is chemically the same as pyrite, but it is lighter in color, grows in a different way, and decomposes much more easily than pyrite does. Use marcasite to help find your way when you are stuck in life, or to help ground yourself when you are feeling out of sorts with your own energy. It is best when carried in your pocket or worn on a piece of jewelry, as this allows you to receive continuous support from it throughout the day.

Moldavite

Moldavite is a deep green crystal that is often used as a talisman for many, as it offers support in connectivity with others. Moldavite is intensely energetic and is said to be able to connect you to the stars and extraterrestrial energies, which can allow you to draw forth energies from anyone at any time. Use moldavite during spiritual healing and discovery journeys, or as a way to communicate with the extraterrestrial energy forces to inquire about various questions you might have about the universe, life, and your mission on earth. Be sure to properly protect yourself to avoid connecting with an unwanted energy force.

Mookaite Jasper

This jasper stone comes in many colors and usually features a flat, matte appearance unless it has been tumbled and shined. This crystal is highly earthy, allowing you to connect with the energies of strength and vitality in a meaningful way. Use mookaite jasper to strengthen your connection to the earth, improve your self-confidence and self-worth, and realize your fullest potential. It is best when worn as jewelry so you can receive continuous support from its energetic forces.

Pinolith

Pinolith is an especially rare crystal that is used to help you achieve the highest state of meditation, while also assisting you with activating your crown chakra. This crystal is often used when one wants to achieve enlightenment and is either increasing their energies or reaching the final stages of enlightenment. With this crystal, you will experience great calming energies, as well as a seemingly deep connection between yourself and everything in the universe around you.

Scolecite

Scolecite is another particularly rare crystal that is known for supporting and activating your heart chakra. It is said that if you sleep with a piece under your pillow, you will experience greater healing and communication abilities. It can also provide you with the opportunity to have a deep, restful sleep. Anytime you are suffering in a relationship with another person, with yourself, or with the universe, use scolecite as a way to gently heal the troubled relationship.

Shungite

Shungite is a more popular yet advanced crystal that is known for its protective qualities. People often use it to purify water of unwanted properties, or to protect themselves from EMF exposure that is caused by technology such as cell phones, computers, smart watches, and other technological devices that emit various digital signals. Wear it as jewelry, keep it in your water, or keep it nearby as a way to protect yourself and your energy field.

Tibetan Tektite

This black stone looks similar to lava stone, though it is different in its chemical makeup. This stone is said to be highly powerful when it comes to healing and activating your chakras, so if you are doing higher chakra work, you can meditate with a piece to greatly activate your chakras. Do not wear it as jewelry or carry it with you long-term unless you are energetically ready to keep your chakras wide open and active for prolonged periods of time. The energy can be intense, especially for those who are not accustomed to being exposed to such high levels of energy.

Chapter 4: The Benefits of Using Healing Crystals

Crystal healing carries with it many benefits beyond the obvious benefits that each individual crystal provides. At one point in history, the perceived benefits included the ability to drive away evil spirits, protect your eternal life, and improve your spiritual wellbeing. These days, there have been reports of many impressive healing benefits beyond the proposed benefits of each individual crystal. Tapping into those benefits by working with crystals is a wonderful way to further improve the quality of life you experience.

The fact that crystal healing is easy, accessible, and can be incorporated with any other healing modality are just some of the perks of crystal healing. This particular healing style can be as advanced or basic as you wish it to be, as it is a largely intuitive healing style that can work in any way you need it to. With the vast array of different crystals available and the many ways to use them, you truly can create and tailor your own protocol for your unique healing needs. In this chapter, we will discuss some of the most profound benefits that creating your own crystal healing protocol can provide.

Work as Supplementary Healing Tools

Healing your spirit, mind, body, and emotions can be an incredibly challenging endeavor, especially when you have to rely on others for your healing experience. While doctors, practitioners, and therapists are all wonderfully skilled at their jobs, there is often one thing lacking: the opportunity to trust in your intuition to guide your healing journey. It is highly valuable and important to include conventional healing methods in your healing journey, as this enables you to effectively treat your symptoms and conditions as needed. However, incorporating crystals into your healing journey means you can take a more personal, hands-on approach where you have the opportunity to trust your intuition and hold some level of control over your wellbeing. Crystal healing can be incorporated with any other healing modality you may be using, whether you are receiving a medical intervention, psychological intervention, energy healing, or anything in between. With crystals, you gain the unique opportunity to actively take part in your own healing journey.

Releases Your Stress and Promotes Relaxation

The very act of working with healing crystals has been known to promote stress relief and relaxation, both of which are valuable when it comes to healing yourself and your body. Stress, in particular, promotes the development of cortisol and adrenaline, which in acute doses, are highly beneficial to your survival. Ongoing stress, however, can lead to the deterioration of your health as the cortisol and adrenaline begin to attack and damage various organs and systems within your body. Through meditating, focusing on your crystals, and directing your intention and your mind, you can create a relaxing space for you to experience relief from excess cortisol and adrenaline.

Are Gentle and Often Peaceful to Work With

Many healing interventions are not gentle, nor peaceful. They can be invasive, overwhelming, and can even cause damage to your body. While they are highly necessary in many different circumstances, there are times where they are not necessary. For example, if you have a spontaneous tension headache, taking an over the counter medicine can be useful, but it can also disrupt the natural harmony within your body. Using crystals, however, is non-invasive and can have the same healing effect, without disrupting the harmony of your natural internal ecosystem.

Deepen Your Understanding of Yourself and the Universe

Crystals are naturally occurring elements of the universe, and they transmit powerful energies, messages, and experiences. When you work with crystals, you deepen your understanding of yourself and the universe as you become more accustomed to working with the subtle energy flow of everything that surrounds you. Once you learn how to tune into and interact with the energies of crystals, it becomes easier to tune into and interact with the energies of everything else around you, too. You start to understand your own subtle energies, the subtle energies of others, and the subtle energies of other things such as the moon phases, seasons, life cycles, plants, animals, and other elements of the natural world. This deepened understanding also deepens your connection to life itself, creating a stronger sense of healing and wellbeing for yourself and all around you.

Provide an Array of Energetic Healing Benefits

As discussed earlier, every crystal has its own unique healing properties. With thousands of minerals existing, most of which can be accessed and used in your personal life, there is no limit on what type of healing you can experience through crystals. If you want to heal aspects of your spirit, mind, emotions, or body, it can all be done with crystals. To get an idea of how vast the world of crystals is, visit a crystal and mineral shop either in person or online to see just a portion of the crystals in existence. You can hold, touch, and research each crystal, which will provide insight into how expansive and powerful this healing modality truly is.

Maximize the Power of Intention and Energy Healing

Energy healing is the "missing link" of healing in most Western healing practices. What many people fail to understand is that your energy is at the root of everything in your life, and if you do not keep your energy right, you are setting the stage for many different illnesses and troubling symptoms to make their way into your life. As you engage in energy healing, crystals can maximize the power of intention and the healing energy itself, allowing you to get even more out of the session. During your energy healing session, be sure to use only one or two types of crystals, or to use many crystals that work toward a similar healing benefit to avoid overwhelming your energy field. With this particular form of energy healing, focusing on just one area at a time is ideal to avoid hectic and inconsistent energies disrupting the healing practice. Slow, relaxing experiences are the point of energy healing and crystal healing alike.

Encourages Intuitive Healing Practices

When you work with crystal healing, you find yourself being encouraged to take part in intuitive healing practices. In the wild, when an animal is sick, they intuitively know what to do to take care of themselves. They will eat specific foods or avoid others, rest more or be cautious in their movements, or otherwise be intuitive about their behaviors. In fact, they are even intuitive about how they deal with their stress. For example, if a gazelle is hunted by a lion and happens to escape the lion, they will thrash excessively until they have fully released the energetic trauma of the experience, then they will go about their daily lives once again. As humans, we are taught to bottle things up, hold it in, and trust in others rather than ourselves, which disconnects us from our intuitive and natural way of being. By engaging in healing practices like crystal healing, you can reconnect with your intuition and play an active, natural role in maintaining your wellbeing.

Chapter 5: Using Crystals to Heal Yourself

Receiving crystal healing yourself is something that can be done either on your own or with the help of a practitioner. Regardless of which route you choose to go, it is important to realize that healing yourself with crystals requires you to understand how crystals work, and to be gentle and patient with yourself during the healing journey. The more patient and gentle you can be, the more open you will be to the experience, and therefore the more powerful your healing experience will be.

Healing Yourself Vs. Hiring a Healing Practitioner

First, you need to consider if you want to do a healing yourself, or with a practitioner. There are pros and cons to both. If you want to heal yourself, you can do so using jewelry, pocket crystals, crystal displays, crystal infusions, or crystal grids. Essentially, you can do everything a crystal healing practitioner can, except you can do it on yourself and as frequently as you need to. You can also adapt your own healing methods to your own needs, allowing you to take a tailored and personal approach to crystal healing.

Healing practitioners are particularly powerful, though, because they remain objective to your experience and can use their extensive knowledge and experience to help you with your healing needs. Further, they will likely have a greater understanding of how to use each crystal, particularly if you are new to this healing modality.

Using Crystal Jewelry for Healing

Crystal jewelry is a powerful healing method you can use that allows you to absorb the healing benefits of your crystals over a long period of time. This is useful with crystals that are not intense, or that bring about benefits you would *want* to experience on an ongoing basis. For example, rose quartz, amethyst, tiger eye, and mookaite jasper are all great for jewelry because they offer benefits that are comfortable to receive over a prolonged period of time. Alternatively, moldavite, lemurian, or Tibetan tektite would be too powerful to be worn as jewelry and would create unwanted energetic experiences if you wore them on your person outside of intentional meditation or intuitive energy sessions.

Pocket Crystals, Crystal Carvings, and Crystal Displays

Pocket crystals, crystal carvings, and crystal displays are all excellent for healing your energy and working with your energy field. Pocket crystals work similarly to jewelry in that you can keep them on your person and use them over long periods of time. You can also place them on your body during meditation sessions.

Crystal carvings and crystal displays can be one and the same, or separate. For example, large crystal carvings could be kept on display, or small display crystals could be held during meditation for crystal healing purposes. Both of these carry powerful benefits. Crystal carvings will carry the meanings of the crystals themselves, as well as whatever symbol was carved into the crystal. Alternatively, crystal displays like spheres, pyramids, or raw crystals also carry their own unique benefits based on the crystal they are and the shape they take on. These crystals can be kept in specific spaces to promote the desired energy benefits in those particular areas. For example, a crystal carving can be kept under your pillow to promote good dreams, or a display crystal could be kept by your front door to prevent negative energy from entering your home.

Facilitating an Objective Healing Experience

When you facilitate a crystal healing session on yourself, there is a certain balance that needs to take place between having an intuitive and personal session and being objective about your healing experience. The intuitive and personal aspect will help you heal your unique needs, or reach your specific desires, while the objective aspect will allow you to objectively channel the energy of the crystal and receive any relevant messages from it.

It can help to facilitate a personal yet objective healing session by creating specific times for each unique type of healing. For example, start the session by setting your personal intentions and taking a moment to personally connect with the crystal, receiving the power of that crystal. Then, move on to staying open to receiving any messages that they crystal might have for you, or that it might be ready to channel to you. After your session, journal on your experiences so you can recall them and examine them later, allowing you to receive the deepest and most complete messages from your session. This way, you receive personal yet objective healing from every crystal healing session you facilitate on yourself.

Healing Yourself and Your Space Properly

Healing yourself and your space properly requires you to follow three simple steps: choose your tools, set your intention, follow your intuition. As you choose your tools, consider what needs or desires you have, and pick the unique crystals that will allow you to meet those goals. Again, either pick just one or two crystals, or pick crystals that work well together with similar goals and purposes to avoid overwhelming your energy field. Next, you need to set your intention. This is where you can decide if you are going to heal your body, your space, or both. You can also decide what type of healing you want to experience and how you want to feel when the session is done. Then, you follow your intuition.

Following your intuition during a healing session means doing what feels right, and this is where you gain the benefit of having intuitive control over your wellbeing. You might hold the crystal, wear it, sleep near it, keep it nearby, keep it in your pocket, polish the crystal, talk to it, rub it over your body, or otherwise work with it to help you gain the benefits of that crystal. There is no "right or wrong" when it comes to using crystals, so long as you are allowing yourself to follow your intuition and experience their value authentically and wholly. The more you allow yourself to follow your intuitive calls, the better your healing session will be.

Chapter 6: Using Crystals to Heal Others

Using crystals to heal others requires intuitive skills that allow you to tap into what type of healing another person needs, and which crystals will help with these ailments. Fortunately, this intuition is already built-in to your soul, so the only skill you need to work on is learning how to listen to it and follow its guidance. Aside from following your intuition, using crystal healing on others is similar to using it on yourself, though there are certain considerations you should take to ensure you have an ethical, comfortable experience.

Your Intuition Meets Crystal Healing

Listening to your intuition enables you to ensure that you have chosen the right crystal for the job. When it comes to crystal healing, the symptoms someone describes to you will not always be the complete list of symptoms they are experiencing. What they often cannot describe lies within their energy field and serves as the root cause of the ailments they are dealing with. These root causes can vary and can subtly shift the way the specific symptoms are experienced, without the individual ever realizing anything has changed.

Through your intuition, you can identify what the individual you are healing is dealing with, so you can pick exactly the right crystals. With crystals, many can cover the same symptoms, but each will heal a specific root cause, so you need to pick exactly the right ones. Beyond simply researching each individual crystal, follow your intuition both when choosing crystals for others, and for yourself.

Checking Crystals Against Each Other

After you have chosen the crystals you will use in a healing session, check them against each other. Ensure your crystals are will work well together to achieve a harmonious healing session. First, check your crystals by looking up their unique meaning to ensure the meanings all align with similar outcomes. Then, keep the crystals near each other for a while and allow your intuition to help you decide whether they feel right together or not. You will know they don't feel right together if you sense a deep nagging or feeling to move some around. You might only need to rearrange them, or you might need to remove certain crystals from the healing collection altogether to get the right energy for your session.

No Contact Without Consent

When you do healing on yourself, you can safely and comfortably massage different body parts with crystals, lay them upon yourself, and otherwise come into contact with yourself. With others, you should never do any of this without consent. Always let the other person know what your specific healing practices are, how you intend on using the crystals, and whether or not they feel comfortable with the specific methods you will be using. If they suggest they are not comfortable with anything, do not try to convince them to become comfortable. Instead, choose a different crystal healing method that eliminates that type of contact so the other person can be comfortable.

It is extremely important that you never make contact without consent for two reasons. First, the person receiving treatment from you deserves to have your utmost respect as they go through a vulnerable healing session. No matter what they may be healing, whether it seems negative or positive in nature, it is a vulnerable moment, and they need to know with absolute certainty that you will respect their space. Second, if you do not respect the other person, their energy will become chaotic and closed around you, making it challenging for them to receive any healing from you in the first place.

Methods for Crystal Healing with Others

All crystal healing methods that you can do on yourself, you can also do on others. You can encourage them to wear specific jewelry or make jewelry unique to their needs. If you advise someone to wear jewelry, encourage them to make a routine for how they put the jewelry on, so that they are open and receptive to the energy in the process. You can also offer them pocket stones, pillow stones, or provide them with decorative stones to keep in their space. The most common modality of crystal healing between a practitioner and client, though, is to have a formal crystal healing session.

Crystal healing sessions generally involve the receiver lying down either on a yoga mat on the floor, or on a massage table so they can be elevated for the practitioner's ease of access. The atmosphere will be set using music, candles, essential oils, incense, decorative crystals, tapestries, low lights, and other pieces that make for a calming environment. When the receiver is relaxed and ready, the healer will often cleanse the aura of the receiver to ensure they are ready to receive the energy of the crystals. Then, they lay a crystal grid around them and allow the individual to meditate with those crystals for several minutes before gently removing the grid and awakening the individual from their meditation.

These types of sessions are strongest, as they provide more acute energy due to the fact that the receiver is open and meditating specifically on those energies, rather than simply having them nearby as they go through their regular day to day routines.

Chapter 7: Crystal Jewelry and Wearables

Crystal jewelry and wearables have become incredibly popular in the past several years. Individuals that are looking to receive support throughout the day from crystal healing will wear bracelets, necklaces, hairpins, and other wearables that allow them to keep the energy of the crystals nearby. While many seem to be doing this as a fashion statement, there is actually a deeper use behind these pieces, and they can provide you with far more than a fashion statement.

How Crystal Jewelry Works

Crystal jewelry works by keeping the energy of a crystal near your body for an extended period of time. The idea is that it subtly and continuously infuses its energy with yours, providing you with the ongoing benefits of that particular crystal. For example, if you were wearing black tourmaline, then any negative energy of the day would be absorbed by the jewelry, rather than by you or your aura.

Technically, crystal jewelry can be worn against any part of your body. However, you do gain most benefits from wearing the crystals in areas of your body that are relevant to the support you need. For example, if you want assistance with communication, you could wear a throat chakra crystal around a necklace, rather than on a bracelet, to get maximum support. Because you are not actively meditating on that crystal throughout the day, keeping it close to the chakra that you need it for will be most effective.

Types of Crystal Jewelry

Crystal jewelry comes in many creative forms. Obvious pieces like necklaces, earrings, rings, and bracelets are available for you to wear. You can also wear barrettes, hair ties or hair forks, belt buckles or belts embroidered with crystal beads, and even clothing accessories that have beads in them. Each type of crystal jewelry has its own unique association and ability, though crystals can be worn anywhere that you feel you need them.

Crystal necklaces are commonly associated with the higher chakras, though their exact association will be based on length. Longer necklaces support the solar plexus and heart chakra, while shorter ones will support the throat, third eye, and crown chakras. Earrings are generally worn for the throat, third eye, and crown chakras, as well, as they are nice and close to these particular parts of your energy field. Crystals that you should wear in this area on a day to day basis include tiger eye, citrine, blue lace agate, labradorite, amethyst, lapis lazuli, clear quartz, and selenite.

Bracelets and rings are excellent for your root, sacral, and solar plexus chakras because they hang nice and close to these chakras. You can wear garnet, black tourmaline, carnelian, pyrite, or yellow calcite in these areas to maximize the flow of energy to your lower chakras.

Barrettes and crystal-infused hairpins are excellent for your third eye and crown chakra. Those who do psychic readings will often wear crystals like lapis lazuli, iolite, celestite, apophyllite, sugilite, moonstone, Herkimer diamond, and lepidolite, which are all great for the third eye and crown chakras.

Belts and other jewelry that can be worn on your hip are best for root chakra crystals like red jasper, smoky quartz, tourmaline, garnet, and bloodstone. These work wonderfully to help protect your energy, and to aid in your survival abilities.

Choosing Your Crystal Jewelry

Choosing crystals to wear as jewelry will require an understanding of what you need, and what feels right for you. There are four things to consider when it comes to picking crystal jewelry: the crystal, what the jewelry is made of, where it is meant to be worn, and what it feels like for you.

Beyond the crystal itself, you need to know what the material that holds the crystal is made out of. Silver, gold, and copper are all great conductors for your crystals. They also have their own unique energetic properties, which will aid in the overall use of the crystal jewelry. Silver is excellent for emotions and the psychic mind, gold is great for balancing and harmonizing, and copper amplifies the natural healing powers of many crystals.

Where the jewelry is meant to be worn will affect how that crystal affects your chakras and your body. Make sure you pick a type of jewelry that will work for your specific needs.

Wearing Crystal Jewelry

Wearing crystal jewelry may seem like a passive experience, especially because of how gentle it can be, but it actually has a major impact on your wellbeing. For this reason, you need to take wearing crystal jewelry as seriously as you take any other form of crystal or energetic healing, as this ensures you get the maximum benefit out of your healing experience.

When you wear crystal jewelry, there are four steps you need to take. First, you need to ensure that your jewelry has been properly charged. We will discuss how to do this shortly. Having your crystals properly charged before wearing them will ensure your crystals are ready to support your energy for the duration of you wearing them.

The second step is to have a unique ritual for putting your jewelry on. Make your ritual intuitively, as this ensures you are open and ready to receive the energy from the crystals. Always do this ritual before putting your jewelry on.

The third step is to keep your jewelry on for as long as you need it. As you wear your jewelry, protect it, care for it, and check in with it from time to time. Touching your jewelry and becoming aware of it helps you keep it within your awareness and routinely open your energy for the jewelry to continue working.

The fourth step to wearing jewelry is taking it off. You should also have a ritual for taking it off that allows you to remove it from your energy field, cleanse it, and place it where it is kept when it is not in use.

Rituals are essential to the healing process of crystal jewelry, so it is important to set a ritual for yourself. If you are unsure of how to create one, you might start by setting an intention when putting your jewelry on and taking it off. From there, your intuition will begin to guide you on the next steps to take, whether it be how you put your jewelry on, or handling it a certain way before putting it on. Always follow your intuition when it comes to energy work, as your intuition knows best.

Maintaining and Caring for Crystal Jewelry

When you are not wearing your jewelry, properly maintaining and caring for it ensures that it is always ready for use. Even if you wear your jewelry daily, maintaining a proper care schedule is important. There are three elements to caring for your crystal jewelry: keeping it clean, cleansing its energy, and storing it properly.

Keeping your jewelry physically clean is important to the wellbeing of your crystal jewelry, partially because this is a way of showing respect to the jewelry, which creates a positive connection between yourself and your crystals. Keeping your jewelry physically clean also ensures that no external energies remain attached to the crystal or the jewelry, possibly dulling its ability to support your wellbeing.

Like raw crystals, crystal jewelry needs to be energetically cleansed to keep it pure and ready to support your aura and energetic wellbeing. You can do this by smudging them with sage, creating a cleansing spray with essential oils, or cleansing them under the moon. Be cautious not to use water or sunlight on your crystals, unless they are crystals which are known for being hardy with either water or sunlight. With some crystals, particularly those that are made of softer minerals, water can cause them to break down, and sunlight can cause them to fade.

Storing your crystal jewelry properly is also important to the wellbeing of your crystals. Aside from preventing your jewelry from breaking, properly storing your jewelry ensures each crystal's cleansed energy remains pure and ready for use. You can store jewelry by hanging it on hooks, keeping it in velvet bags, or otherwise keeping them separate.

Chapter 8: Crystal Grids and Body Grids

Crystal grids and body grids are a powerful way to channel the energy of crystals and direct the energy of the universe. Both of these crystal healing methods can be used with healing, manifesting, and otherwise directing energy as per your needs. Like all other forms of crystal healing, your intuition plays a large role in your ability to heal using crystals. Aside from that, you also need to have five other steps in place to ensure that you gain maximum benefit from your crystals, which we will be covering in this chapter.

Set Your Energetic Healing Intention

Before you can commence any healing session with gridwork, you need to set your energetic healing intention. Your intention will calibrate your intuition so it can guide you through the entire process. With gridwork, you will set your intention before even deciding which healing method you will use, or which supplies you will use for your grid.

Setting your intention starts with knowing what is "off" in your energy field, so you are aware of what needs to be healed. It may help to hold yourself open to receiving guidance over a few days, as what you genuinely need may not be obvious at first. Keeping your intuition open ensures that you develop a deeper awareness of what you need, and what specific intention you should set for your healing session.

Once you have identified your desired intention, give yourself enough time to clarify the intention, and summarize it in a few words or a single sentence at most. This intention will be kept for the duration of your healing experience so you can infuse it in every step of the healing process. Creating a mantra from your intention can make the process of infusing your intention into the healing experience easier.

Some great mantras you might like to try include:

- "I attract healing in all ways, always."
- "I heal my ability to manifest with ease."
- "I open myself to receive healing."
- "I create wholeness from within."
- "I heal a protected aura."

When making your intention mantras, always start with the word "I" and speak in the present tense. This way, you are attracting your desires *right now,* rather than rooting them in the past or future.

Decide on a Crystal Grid or Body Grid

Crystal grids and body grids are similar in nature but are built differently. Crystal grids are generally built on a surface and are meditated over, while body grids are built over your physical body. Each has its own uses and benefits, and can support your healing in specific ways, so pick the one that best reflects your healing needs.

Crystal grids can be made on tapestries, grid sheets, tabletops, the floor, or any other surface you have. Many healers will pick a surface specific to the healing they need. For grounding experiences, they might set their grid upon the forest floor, whereas for elevating or manifesting experiences, they may use a tapestry infused with specific colors or energy. Crystal grids draw a great amount of energy into one specific space and direct the energy in a certain flow, based on the way the crystals have been laid out. A significant benefit is that you can keep the crystals in place for extended periods of time, allowing the energy to grow and flow for much longer. Many healers will create a grid under the full moon and let it sit until the new moon, or the next full moon, giving the energy plenty of time to grow.

Body grids are laid out over your body. They are not as long-lasting as crystal grids are, though they do hold significant power. Because they are laid against your body, you can directly receive the energy and hold it within your energy field. Always ensure you set aside enough time to meditate with your grid so you can receive the energy long enough for it to have an impact.

As well, set your body grid from your feet up to your head, so you are not disrupting the crystals once they have been set. Body grids are also great when you are doing crystal healing for someone else, as you can set them over their body and have them meditate to receive acute energy from the healing session.

Gather Your Crystals and Supplies

With your intention clear, you can now focus on gathering the supplies for your crystal grid or body grid. If you are laying a crystal grid, look for a place to lay your grid, whether that be a specific point on the ground or on a crystal grid tapestry. If you are doing a body grid, create a space for you to lay down and build the grid upon yourself. Aside from location, there are two other factors to consider: the atmosphere, and the crystals.

The atmosphere for your environment is important to the healing, as it can either benefit the healing or take away from it. A calm, relaxing environment that allows you to feel warm and open will assist you with receiving the energy from your grid, while an environment that is distracting or uncomfortable will take away from your ability to receive that energy. You can create a calm, relaxing environment by heading out into nature, or by surrounding yourself with calming music, candles, incense, essential oils, low lighting, and anything else that can support you in feeling at peace in your space.

As you gather crystals, look for ones that will sit well in a grid. You want crystals that have the right energy, work together well, and that will sit nicely on your grid. If you are using a crystal grid, small crystal chips, tumbled stones, points, and smaller raw crystals are all excellent for the grid. Many healers will purchase multiples of different types of stones to maximize the energy and draw forth as much intention as possible. If you are using a body grid, larger, flatter crystals that have been tumbled are ideal so they can rest comfortably against different parts of your body. Crystal wands are also great, as they can help point energy in certain directions within your aura, elevating your healing experience in those specific spots where it is most needed.

Choose the Time for Your Healing Session

Picking the right time for your healing session is important, though it is not necessary. While a healing session can be conducted at any time, there are certain times that will draw forth more energy than others. There are two factors with regards to time that you should consider; the time of day, and the celestial time.

For the time of day, morning sessions are wonderful for drawing in fresh, renewing energy, while evening sessions are wonderful for relaxation and peace. In the morning, you can elevate your energy and bring that with you throughout the day, while in the evening you can release any energy you have carried throughout the day. Later evening sessions are great for manifesting, as you will be going to bed afterward, which means you will be completely at peace and open to allowing the energy to continue percolating in your system, without being distracted by day to day events.

Celestial times are also good to consider. The moon phase is one way you can time your grid healing session. The full moon is a wonderful time to manifest or draw more energy into your system, while the new moon is a wonderful time to release energy or cleanse your system. You can also consider the zodiac or look for other unique celestial events. Specific zodiac seasons, eclipses, meteor showers, and other planetary alignments make for excellent healings under different circumstances. If you desire to do a particularly strong or powerful healing session, look for the celestial event that corresponds with the type of healing you are doing, and time your healing during that event. The power will be magnified, and your results will be far more significant.

Conduct Your Healing Session

The final thing to do is actually conduct your healing session. As long as you have done the previous steps properly, your only focus will be on what you are doing. If you intend to conduct many grid healing sessions, you might want to create a ritual for how you conduct your sessions. This ritual can be determined based on what your intuition feels is right. Each ritual should have five aspects: the setup, drawing in energy, holding energy, releasing energy, and the take down.

The setup can be completed by setting up the space for your grid, including the atmosphere itself as well as the grid. Drawing in energy is achieved by meditating over the grid and allowing it to accumulate as much energy as possible, so you can amplify the energy in that space and prepare it for gridwork. Holding energy allows you to receive the amplified energy and let it be directed through your energy field. The process of holding the energy is generally the longest part of the healing. Releasing energy allows you to release the energy of the healing session, and it is necessary for the success of the session. When you release energy, you are releasing the healing session itself, while the healed and healing energies will continue to stay in your space long after the session ends. Lastly, the takedown is when you cleanse and put away all of your materials so they can be safely stored. This is important, as it prevents energy from sitting out and becoming stagnant or, being misdirected and disrupting your energy field after a positive healing session.

It is a good idea to set aside at least two hours, if not more, for a healing session. The longer you have, the easier it will be to give yourself plenty of time to invest in each specific stage of healing. You never want to feel rushed during a healing session, as this can leave your session incomplete and can result in you receiving less potent energetic support. Once a session is complete, always plan on giving yourself space to "come down" from the session, as your energy may feel altered for a while afterwards. Calming activities, or activities related to the healing itself, will give you the opportunity to let that energy integrate as you go back into your daily routine.

Chapter 9: Crystal Space Clearing and Healing

Crystals are commonly used for personal energy healing; however, they can be used for setting the energy of certain spaces, too. If you want to know just how powerful crystals are to an environment, visit a crystal cave, or even a Himalayan salt cave. The energy of these spaces is magnificent and proves how powerful crystals are to the environment around them.

When you set crystals up in your environment with the purpose of clearing or healing the environment, it is important that you have the right understanding of what you are doing. When you are healing an individual, it is obvious that you would view that individual as an entity and treat them as an entity. When you are healing a space, you must learn how to hold the same energy and perspective over the space as you would an individual. This space has its own signature energy and behaves in its own unique way. Viewing it as an individual entity allows you to treat that individual energy appropriately and create your desired results with it.

Anytime you are working with the energy of a space, you must also consider the existing energy of that space and the other energies being introduced to that space. Each environment will have its own unique "feel," which can be identified by simply walking into that space and keeping yourself open to receiving that feeling. You might not be able to describe the feeling or summarize what it is, but you will be able to recognize it within yourself. Discovering the energies passing through the environment, or the energies belonging to the people and animals in that space will also help you determine what energies you should factor in when working with that space. High traffic environments with many bodies passing through will often need more intense crystals, while those which are only experienced by a few people can handle less intense crystals. Keeping the right amount of crystals in a space, and the right energies, will ensure you get your desired results from that space.

Choosing Crystals for Your Space

When you know the environment you are working with, and the energies passing through it, choosing the crystals for your space is easy. You want to choose crystals that will help balance the energy of the environment, while also promoting the energies you desire from that environment. For example, let's say you are setting up crystals in your living room. This space is frequented by your whole family and may be a space where people come to after a long, stressful day. Crystals that absorb negative energies and promote relaxing energies, then, would balance out the energy of the room and support the energy of your environment.

Crystals for your environment come in all shapes and sizes. Some of the crystal arrangements you might find include:

- Bowls of smaller crystals
- Crystal bowls
- Crystal figurines or statues
- Medium raw, tumbled, or cut crystals
- Large raw, tumbled, or cut crystals
- Crystal lights and lamps
- Crystal wall decor
- Window hangings and mobiles made of crystals
- Crystal wire wrapped trees
- Crystal furniture
- Crystal balls

There is an abundance of crystals in every shape and form you can possibly think of. They come in nearly every type of crystal, every size, and with many different uses. Just as you would with conducting a healing session on yourself, it is important that you carefully consider each crystal and choose only those that will promote greater healing in your environment. Never pick crystals that conflict with each other's energy, and also avoid having too many different types of crystals in any one space as this can overwhelm the energy field. Even if they all generally do the same thing, the subtle differences can become overwhelming and result in you having difficulty with maintaining the energies in that space.

Setting Crystals Up in Your Environment

As you arrange crystals in your environment, there are many things to consider. The crystals themselves, the energetic flow of your environment, and the desires of the crystal should all play into the final resting place of each piece. The overall decorative look of your environment should be the last thing you consider, as these crystals are more of a tool than a decorative piece, though they will happily serve both purposes.

The crystals themselves need to be considered based on what type of crystal they are, what design they are, and where they make the most sense in your environment. Naturally, you don't want to have a lamp tucked away in an obsolete space, or a large geode piece in the center of your room. Consider what pieces would make the most sense for your environment.

Your environment already has an energetic flow, regardless of what crystals are or aren't in your environment. Everything you add to your environment, and how you add it, will affect the energy of your environment. When placing crystals in your environment, you can either work with the existing energy flow or redo the energy flow if a new energy flow would work better for that space. In an environment where you are already satisfied with the flow, the crystals will be used to amplify that energy or add additional energy that will work in harmony with the space. In a space where the energy flow is undesirable, you can arrange the crystals to adjust the energetic flow to one that is more desirable.

Finally, you need to consider the desire of each crystal. Often, crystals will "communicate" with you through your intuition to tell you where they want to be placed. If a crystal continually "tells" you that it wants to be placed in a specific space, it is a good idea to oblige as it will work its energy best in that unique space in your environment.

Crystal Wands for Healing Your Space

If you feel the energy of your space has been particularly disturbed, you can always conduct a specific healing session for that space. The easiest way to conduct a healing session on your space is to use crystal wands, as crystal wands can allow you to point and direct energy through your environment.

Crystal wands come in many different forms, shapes, and sizes, so you can pick the one that best fits your space. To conduct your healing, start in the northern side of your room and wave the wand around your space as if you were washing the energy clean. Work in a clockwise motion, waving the wand over every corner, window, nook, and cranny as you go. Take your time in areas where the energy feels heavy, or in areas where others' energy frequently passes through, to ensure you effectively cleanse away all unwanted energies. You are done when you come back to the north corner. You may want to pass through the space with different wands to cleanse, heal, and set the energy.

Crystal-Infused Room Sprays

Another way to cleanse your space is to use crystal-infused room sprays. Create a crystal-infused room spray by soaking crystals in water to infuse their energy into the water. Ensure you are using crystals that will not break down or become damaged in the water, and that will not introduce toxic elements to the water. If you want to create a more advanced room spray, you might also add essential oils or use a celestial event to help you charge the water.

An excellent room spray "recipe" you can use is:

- 1 Large Chunk Rose Quartz
- 1 Large Chunk Fluorite
- ¾ Cup Purified Water
- ¼ Cup Witch Hazel
- 10 Drops Lavender Oil
- 10 Drops Rosemary Oil
- 10 Drops Spearmint Oil

Start your room spray under the full moon. Place your purified water in a glass bowl and put the rose quartz and fluorite in the water. Leave it for at least 24 hours or for an entire moon cycle, depending on what you have time for. When the water is infused, remove the crystals and pour it into a spray bottle. Add the witch hazel, then the essential oils. Shake the bottle before spraying it to ensure the oils are properly infused with the spray.

If you find the aforementioned spray is too sticky, you can always swap witch hazel for alcohol. However, you will need to be careful as alcohol can stain and damage certain materials. If you are unsure, do a spot test on hidden parts of furniture or your carpet to check for staining, and keep your room spray away from furniture or materials that stain.

Chapter 10: Taking Care of Your Crystals

Taking care of your crystals is an important part of having healing crystals in the first place. Caring for your crystals will optimize their energy, keep them pure, and will increase the connection you feel with your crystals. Having a strong connection with your crystals ensures that you gain maximum benefit from them for the same reason having a strong connection with your friends increases the value you gain from those relationships. When you know what your crystal's energy is, and what that crystal is capable of, you discover far more ways to use it. You also genuinely enjoy having it around, sitting in its presence, and receiving healing energy from it. Even if you are looking at several different pieces of the same crystal, you might find that you connect better with one piece over the other. Always go for the piece you connect better with, as this is the piece that will work best in your energy field.

Maintaining your crystals can be seen as a relationship-building activity with your crystals. As you cleanse and store them, you spend time in their presence and them in yours. Some people even talk to or sing to their crystals, and find that they grow rather fond of them, as though their crystals are a sort of "friend."

Crystal Cleansing Sprays

One way to maintain your crystals is to create a crystal cleansing spray. The best crystal cleansing spray is made with clear quartz and sage. You should use the crystal cleansing spray in the same way you would use a room spray, though you still must avoid using it around crystals that dissolve in water as you can damage those crystals. A crystal cleansing spray is particularly handy for crystal jewelry or other daily use pieces because it allows you to have a relatively quick ritual for cleansing the jewelry before putting it on and after taking it off. While you never want to rush your crystal experiences, it is also reasonable that you do not want to spend hours upon hours on certain rituals, especially those that you perform daily.

To make a crystal cleansing spray with quartz and sage, fill a small spray bottle with clear quartz chips and cover them with purified water. If you have fresh sage leaves, add them to the water, otherwise use 10-15 drops of sage essential oil. If you use the essential oil, always shake vigorously before spraying to ensure the essential oil is mixed in with the water, as it will not dissolve in the water. Then, spray your crystals from about 10-12 inches away to ensure they are misted but not soaked. You can leave the crystals, and fresh sage leaves in your spray long-term with this particular spray.

Smoke Cleansing Your Crystals

Smoke cleansing is both a spiritual practice and a practical practice. Science has shown that smoke creates an acidic environment, which means it has antibacterial properties for anything it comes into contact with. Spiritually, smoke is said to cleanse the aura and energy of anything it comes into contact with, and smoke from specific plants can cause certain energies to become present. To use smoke cleansing on your crystals, you want to burn sage incense and run your crystals through the smoke to cleanse them. You will know when the crystals are properly cleansed because they will *feel* cleansed. Once they are, you can set them down in their storage space. It is a good idea to use smoke cleansing on your crystals at least once a month to provide a "deep" cleansing for your crystals.

Moonlight Cleansing Methods

Moonlight is a powerful cleanser, as is sunlight. Most crystals will thrive in moonlight as it provides a gentle, cleansing energy while also charging crystals, so they become more pure and powerful. Sunlight, on the other hand, is not quite as simple because certain crystals will lose their color under the sunlight. Rose quartz, for example, will lose its pink coloration if you leave it in the sun for too long. To cleanse your crystals under the moonlight, place them out under the full moon and the new moon. Ideally, you want to place them out under both moon phases every month. The full moon will charge your crystals, while the new moon will release any unwanted energies from your crystals. Sunlight charges and cleanses all at once.

To ensure the moonlight is able to have the biggest impact on your crystals, it is best to put them directly outside. You might place them on a tray or in a shallow bowl and place that surface out under the moonlight. While you can place them in the window or in a covered container outside, doing so can result in you blocking out some of the moon's energy. Allowing your crystal to sit directly under the full and new moon ensures it gets the most direct energy, thus maximizing the moon's ability to cleanse and charge your crystals.

Checking the Energetic Charge

Once you have cleansed a crystal, you can check the energetic charge of that crystal. This is not entirely necessary after a cleansing, but it does allow you to determine whether or not the crystal is properly cleansed and ready for use. You should always check the energetic charge before using a crystal.

To check the energetic charge of a crystal, close your eyes, take a few cleansing breaths, and hold the crystal in your hand. A fully charged crystal should *feel* charged in your hand. You should feel your hand warming up, and a significant amount of energy should start pulsing through your hand from the crystal. If you are using a crystal that is generally gentler in nature, such as rose quartz or selenite, it may feel overwhelmingly calm in your hand when you hold it. This "overwhelming" energy is a sign that the crystal is ready for use.

If you begin wearing or using a crystal and it feels as though you are not receiving energy from that crystal, or you are not receiving the right energy from it, you should set it aside so it can be cleansed and charged again. Some crystals that have been heavily used may require a few full cleansing cycles to totally recover from heavy use.

Storing Your Crystals

There are three "rules" for storing your crystals. Following these rules ensures their energy remains pure, they remain protected, and they continue to work when you are ready to use them. You should follow these rules every time you store your crystals.

The first rule for storing your crystals is to always store them away from where you want to sleep or relax. Keeping your crystals away from areas where specific energy must be used, especially areas where you want to sleep or relax, ensures that they do not mess with your energy field when you are trying to enjoy down time.

The second rule is to keep like-crystals together. This means keeping the same type of crystal together, while also keeping crystals with the same uses or meanings together. Avoid mixing and mingling your crystals in their storage space, as it can make the space overwhelming and can disrupt the energetic charge of your crystals.

The third rule is to ensure that each crystal has been respected. It should be stored in a way that does not lead to it becoming dirty, chipped, or otherwise damaged.

The best ways to store your crystals include laying them out on a tray, storing them in a shallow silver or glass bowl, laying them out on a piece of clear quartz, or keeping them in leather or velvet sachets. Each of these storage methods will keep them ready for use.

Preparing Your Crystals for Use

If your crystals have been in storage, you will need to prepare them for use. To prepare your crystals for use, bring them out of storage and prepare a deep cleansing ritual for them, so they are fully prepared to support your energy field. Start by using a simple smoke cleansing process, then lay your crystals out under the moonlight for them to be cleansed and charged by the moonlight. If they have been in storage for a long time, leave them from the beginning of the new moon to the end of the full moon. Before you use those crystals in a ritual, use a cleansing spray on them. By properly cleansing your crystals after they have been stored, you effectively pour love and energy into them so they can pour love and energy back into you. This way, you nurture your connection with your crystals and gain maximum healing energy from your crystals each time you use them.

Conclusion

Congratulations on completing *Crystal Healing!*

This book was written to support you in discovering the power of crystal healing. Crystal healing is an ancient healing art that has been used for everything from healing physical ailments to spiritual disturbances. People have also used it to heal their ability to manifest, attract their desires, and unlock their full spiritual abilities.

I hope that by reading *Crystal Healing,* you were able to uncover the magnificent power of crystals, and the value they can add to your life. There are many different ways you can heal yourself with crystals, ranging from jewelry to decor, and even room sprays or body sprays. Using crystals is as much about intention and technique as it is about the crystal itself, making crystal healing a highly engaged form of healing. Rather than passively sitting back and receiving the energy from each crystal, you gain more value by actively working with the crystals to receive the benefits they offer.

Now that you have reached the end of this book, I encourage you to take the opportunity to conduct a crystal healing session on yourself or your space. So long as you follow the steps in this book and remain highly intentional about what you are doing, you will find yourself enjoying a powerful healing experience. You have exactly what it takes to conduct a proper healing session already built-in to your intuition, so follow what feels right, and you will be sure to have a positive experience.

You might be incredibly excited to get to work with your crystals, but I caution you against going too fast. Avoid accumulating your crystals too quickly or attempting to do too much at once, as both of these things can lead to overwhelm. You should feel a personal connection to each crystal you acquire, and you should always provide yourself with ample time to integrate the energy from each healing session before moving on to your next one. This way, you receive the maximum benefit from each session, and you do not overwhelm your energy field with the crystals you are using.

Finally, I'd like to thank you for taking the time to read this book. I hope you have found it both enjoyable and informative, and I wish you the best of luck on your spiritual journey!